Praise for
The Syndicate of Water & Light

Marc Vincenz unbalances ideas ⋯⋯⋯⋯ ⋯ ⋯ that he might restore a lost carriage throu.. ...age, intelligence, and all the right words. I am describing here what the syndicate of elements demands of a writer who chooses to be as gifted as his most special reader. This is a very sweet manuscript and a brave book.

—Norman Dubie

In poems with vivid imagery, arresting, delightful juxtapositions and agile lines, Marc Vincenz manages a series of discussions—arguments, even—concerning the relationships, evanescent and problematic, between seeing and naming, nature and the struggle of reason against itself. These poems are about proposition and perception, the balance we all manage daily between the pleasures we take in our experiences of the natural world and our concern for the threats it suffers. For Vincenz, the cosmologies we have contrived and the myths that sustain them have opened spaces where industrial exploitation and degradation thrive. Despite the vivid sense of ecological hazard, its toxicity and long shadows, there is a redeeming attention here to physical detail. In a late section of the book, poems, very much at ease with nature and natural experience, are generated, quite deliberately, under the aegis of a series of computer-like codes, reminding us that richly detailed experience exceeds the arbitrary and contrived, however useful they might seem. Vincenz's *The Syndicate of Water & Light* proposes an available mystery for the self in a fragile world— how language, which has been complicit in the loss we see around us, can reclaim in poetry a primary and enduring sense of what we experience.

—Michael Anania

In *The Syndicate of Water & Light,* traveling through the center of the Earth, Marc Vincenz navigates the fundamental powers of poetic language, a questioning which leads through confrontation, dialectic, and eventually acceptance—opening luminescent tracts to epiphany and enlightenment. In interrogating our complex sense of self-in-world, Vincenz is both a see-er and a seer. This is a modern vision of Dante's afterlife, perhaps as the afterlife of the Earth herself. An extremely worthwhile allegorical journey with vast rewards.

—Maxine Chernoff

"Here is a tribe who has been to paradise / and heard unspeakable words." In Marc Vincenz's newest collection, he explores a chronological arc, from the distant past to the future. He leads the reader into "uncharted territory / through which the small mind traverses." By turns, prayer-like and unrelenting, the poet reveals a binary "othermind." Vincenz questions notions of humanity, suggesting that codes have driven us throughout history. In a holographic future, he imagines a pastoral virtual reality. Stringent words create the poetry of synthesis—human and AI. Ultimately, these cells cluster and reemerge as a new sentient voice, which charts our species' need for transformation and rebirth. Far from being artificial, Vincenz's intelligence is a laboratory in which language is electrified and brought back to life.

—Dean Kostos

The Syndicate of Water & Light

The Syndicate of Water & Light

A Divine Comedy

Marc Vincenz

with an afterword
by Robert Archambeau

Station Hill

BARRYTOWN

Published by Station Hill of Barrytown, the publishing project of the Institute of Publishing Arts, Inc., 120 Station Hill Road, Barrytown, NY 12507, New York, a not-for-profit, tax-exempt organization [501(c)(3)].

Online catalogue: www.stationhill.org
e-mail: publishers@stationhill.org

Cover image: *Storm in a Tea Pot* (2016), Marc Vincenz

Library of Congress Cataloging-in-Publication-Data

Name: Vincenz, Marc, 1966– author, editor, translator
Title: The Syndicate of Water & Light / Marc Vincenz
Description: Barrytown, NY : Station Hill Of Barrytown, 2018
Identifiers: LCCN 2017040263 / ISBN 978-1-58177-168-8
Classification: LCC PS3622.I538 A6 2018 | DDC 811/.6—dc23
LC record available at http://lccn.loc.gov/2017040263

Manufactured in the United States of America

The language that comes
with matter
is the matter that comes
with language.

Lost in the Z

OS ∞

When the past is always with you,
it may as well be present;
& if it is present,
it will be future as well.

—William Gibson, *Neuromancer*

Prologue: From Our Ancestors' Spaceship

For more things are sought than found, they said.
And after the fires of desire and delusion

have been extinguished, observe the change
of the roll and the pitch of the wave.

What were the sources of our impulse?
The what-we-don't-know-we-don't-yet-know?

On those endless sidepaths, beware the obstacles
of recollection and the immutable errors of knowledge.

Here is a tribe who has been to paradise
and heard unspeakable words. They called them

a natural interrogative—the promises of something
that shaped itself in the making or was simply consumed

in whirling tongues of fire. We always constructed
our own cosmologies—and never forget, things are not

what a language names them. Is not the cruel commander
also the faithful husband? or the resourceful hero,

the lying con man? is not the He-in-search-
of-his-identity also the Everyman?

From the surface of an unpeopled world
we followed knowledge like a sinking star, far

behind a sun where islands rising out of the sea
were hammered in waves of unlimited time.

Imagine strong stories that grant immortality,
where in their particular chasm, cheaters and flatterers

whisper themselves back into the past—
all this, long before the first chronicle of travel,

before the first account of war,
when there was still that quality of déjà vu.

Where a Dark Bird Flourishes

How the Story Begins

Language, Michelle said, was created
by positive deductions contrary

to our thinking, this uncharted territory
through which the small mind traverses.

I am, said she, a bee gathering pollen
not to make honey, but to buy time.

Charles' imagination was the instrument
of evolution—to conceive that which

occurred even before it actually arose.
Perhaps though, as François surmised,

they were all just merchants of
each other's small infinity of light.

& they wandered astonished
through the market stalls of a small city

made of jumbled words. Future
was a place that fastened the tail-end

of all potential stories, imaginary
voyages where the boat is a needle

& the compass the sky. How
they wished to learn what might lie

beyond their last breath in
the descent to the underworld

of the self, & what currency
of words might still be left behind.

The Market Dynamics of a Silent Sea

1) An

impenetrable thicket
of pipes & tubes
of valves & bolts & flanges

& meters & dials pushing red,
of scaffolding & metal tanks
& columns of distillation bleeding

runoff into groundwater,
of effluents sweeping a paper-thin sky
where charred catwalks crisscross

an iced horizon & micro motes
carry an atomic feedback loop
built on cotton & salt & indigo & lime,

on synthesized feedstocks
& rayon & ersatz dyes
& those life-giving pulses sputter

modified seeds onto a dampened breeze
where descendants of slaves share
the fenceline & the precedent

of monopoly pickets a future
where grounded research continues
into the shifting states of an Otherworld.

2) Or,

a social milieu artificial or
contrived where contraband
is easily monied & that higher-calling

of hydrocarbons is mapped within
loose strands of muffled vocal cords,
here our table wobbling under polyester flowers

or that faux fruit shimmering
on linoleum & the polyethylene tablecloths
fluttering a red & white checkered cotton

of olden French country cousins.
There the chemical fingerprints
where the origin of cancers beyond

the knowledge of science or
the market dynamics of a silent sea
surge in a self-preserving tide

where Land becomes the iron hand
of the Othermind & Wild is served on time
in expired, bloated tin cans.

A Cipher

... for these roses [are] weighted with passion
perfectly and correctly allow themselves
to be decomposed into roses and passion ...
—Roland Barthes

How could they have been defined, when
reaching for a reflection, the mind

was rudely battered by a thrust of ineffable vision?
Where did the book vanish and carry off all the detail?

or, is this the same story even though
it looks quite different on the page.

All that speech made visible, all the sound
contrition of the heart, a confession of deadly sins

and a strange capacity to imagine in order to feel.
Ah, here it lies eroded by slight of tongue, rogue

thoughts as knots on a string, the dead conversing
in bullet points across myopic centuries.

How else could they make a rose bloom again
from its very ashes. Every page may be an oracle

in amorous entanglement—and yet, the first lines
were not songs of love, but checklists of things,

of grain and livestock, of tiles now turned to dust.
Perhaps we should follow the tracks of their creatures

across the pastures to reach the end, or perhaps,
just perhaps, we prefer to be passionately lost.

The Pretense of a Conclusion

To strive, to seek, to find
and [never] to yield.
　　　　—Tennyson

Argument Z.

M i r r o r s of what
we don't yet see,

a desire to
know, like being

present at
your own birth, & then—

the primordial muscle
lodged in your throat,

that tells you
to be in time, or to be

in space, or—better,
to be

in both
at the same time.

Argument Y.

Hallucinations pro-
jecting into

a future, yet
somehow sensing

the prickle
of an inherent paradox,

the je-ne-sais-quoi
of a liquid state—

questions conjured up
in a nest of spirits.

Argument X.

Did we believe
what we were told?

or, did we assume
there was a sub-

versive subplot
of pastiches, of

colorful catalogues
& fancy parodies,

where the place
of everything

was actually
in its antipodes?

Argument W.

Is that why we
scorned those

wandering
pedagogues even

when eternity
surrounded

every single
quivering note?

An Earth of Broken Dreams:

—after Dante

"On the one hand, seamless:

that snowglobe of
re-shaken
history:"

> Groping in an alphabet soup,
> your mind is stuck—then struck
> by lightning:

an hypothesis
becomes a flash flood:

> behind the glass
> there is no world beyond
> our verbal capacities:

perhaps the experience is lost
in an attempt to mother it:

> those vast oceans before language
> & time approaching something
> coming into being:

Maybe the color of my eyes
changes from moment to moment:

are *we* who we are when
none of our cells are the same
as when we first touched down?

Isn't everything, even that me,
just another metaphor of itself?

    & what is that desire
    to know who we are by recalling
    who we might have been?

Don't we need to see things
in order to name them?

    Jung called them back-
    ward-looking dreams or
    forward-looking anticipations:

unrequited words
as yet unrecited:

    Is there not a place
    we know exists without
    having landed on it?

That long struggle of reason
against reason guided:

by some unknown hand
under the whirling intensity
of an uninterrupted sky:

Or, do all actions
determine our geography?

Isn't it visible
in the stones & in the stars,
deep in the love of the divine:

Or the oaks' *contrapasso*—
those that have
tumbled

through the cracks of countless ages
& their acorns rotting
on wasted lands:

drawing circles & paths
from one intersection to another:

giving an illusion that we are
somewhere here,
just by advancing the conversation:

& precisely *here:* subdued forests
where a wolf howls

    & an obscene bird
    of night chatters
    incessantly:

"On the other hand, condemned:

to whisper *forever*
into the snow
into the snow ..."

Dirty Talk

Were these sentimental effusions
outbursts of thirst? last wishes?

The pain that may have gnawed them
in the end, transformed by love?

by intense pleasures?
Were they surrounded by

borrowed objects, by a catalogue of kisses—
always the guest & never the host?

Here we are: an alien climbs
unfamiliar stairs in a semblance

of love, feeling the past
in the warm sputter of drizzle.

Is our identity forfeit beyond
what language shows of Troy's,

of Rome's succulent heroes?—
or, any other god-held truth

handed on by a relay of priests
& a theater of patriarchs?

First thought: Incomprehension.
A whiff of invisible subtleties,

of implicit connotation, scientific
jargon & children's babble

from orthodox theology &
the language of dreams streaming

into the subverted & reinforced,
then reduced to bare essentials.

Here is where the dog enters
the poem & circles my feet.

Dropping a Bomb on the Louvre

Here in the forest by the creek,
like the skull of a small mammal
polished by insects & rain,
enveloped in loaded silence, a gun.

Are the screams across the water,
simply the neighbors quarreling?
Is anybody watching?

As long as hope retains
that trace of ocean green, it sweeps
away all the other voices.

A cipher taken on blind faith, perhaps.

As between two lovers, like a dollar bill
that holds no reality beyond its face, the currency
offers great reward to a vibrant imagination.

When did the god of faith become the god
of hard cash? All those schemes, extracting
sunshine from the purgatory of earth.

Literal or allegorical, mystical or demagogical,
but pierced through with a million sorrows.

A desire for things that are of this world
in avaricious hands, bursting forth to weigh
& clutch & hang their greatest worth.

Passages from the Underground

A Final Gathering

Filling up stolen time
with bids &

deceptions, with
an evening sky

flowing into
the house—

it is lovely
to see

above the city
in the flight

of the snow geese,
valor surpasses

honorable exile—
still, the party continues

& the street noise
winds down,

beneath the sniffles
& the coughs &

that faint voice enduring
murky suspicions.

I might be thinking
we are divided

like thieves, when
a trembling pre-

monition that things
are void

of substance, suddenly
washes over me.

Sunset

Has the world
been spared?

The rotten teeth—
simplicity, objects fixed

on false privileges,
reality like stones,

memories like sea,
the secret key

that may have been
written, a barren

terrain, where light
draws streaks

in clouds, long-
suffering alleyways,

cardboard feet,
the puddles, loud-

mouthed assault
of the multitude.

Shimmering smoke.
Toxic time, the city's

edge, a burden—
beyond the horizon,

behind a barbed-wire
fence, some-

thing useless, some-
thing tossed away.

Reflections

No more
to be heard,

the daylight
moon, sizing

up destinies,
faces grow

haggard in
frail windows—

the declaration
of a secret.

Knight of Cups,
the Fool, Seven

of Denari—
the dark

loyalty, self-
pity, re-

proach. The King
lies face-

down, ex-
pired by

the fountain,
as a crow

plucks through
his robes—

but where, where
the crown?

The Language of Dawn

Bold water
mirroring the sky,

modest dreamer
of elephant clouds,

amorous arms,
vaulted books

of symbols
within symbols—

the faces dissolve.

An Epilogue & a Prologue

Forewarned.
I knew it.

The meaning
in the music,

fateful atoms
vibrating against

the blue-washed
wall, the shadow

of the leaping
deer flashing

across the eye
& the face

of a loved one
in a world

beyond corruption …
where the music

flies in that last
afternoon when

I tread with
the shadows,

opening my throat
to be present.

If, When

The never-ending
scribble, then

that smoothing-
down of the sun,

the weight of the
reality of words

never to be read;
forgetfulness,

language woven
with rivers & skies,

great plains traversed
where the wild

flourishes, leaps
& bounds

in its own bounty.
Here, the murmur

of the crowds,
the flicker

of silvered tongues,
when, once again,

that smoothing-
down of the sun,

the afternoons with
alternate endings

where the maze
of buildings

become tangled
woodland, floating

in a sea of music,
and deep

in the center,
a field of yellow

flowers raise
theirs heads toward

the light

Eclipse

The past intrudes
with its old habits

when the breeze enters
carrying with it the deeds

annulled. Is this a flaw
of nature? A sense

that nothing truly departs?
The residue, the whispers

all wear the past,
still harboring vestiges

of ancient meteorites
that fell from exploding stars.

Observe the lizard stock-still
on his rock, creatures

clinging to the shore,
as if the next incursion

may be the last suffocation
in the eternal face of the sky.

All that was, isn't, will never.
Go on. Move.

Soar. Fly.

Evanescent

To leave nothing
but fingerprints,

fragments, mist—
a relief what happens

after that, the integrity
of a downfall, then to go

back into the bark, become
the subtitle, the good manners

of subversive words laughing
in the middle of the night.

To be suspended belief
in the cradle of a dream—

a semblance, or bones
walking into the void

Cold Blood

The stream
that bares them,

the visible/invisible
dizzy with sunlight,

stilted, graceful,
sweet-skinned, steaming,

hissing, sober/drunk,
nodding to themselves,

to the water, to the wind,
perched sideways

on a branch
of light

Spirit King

White air wisps,
dancing shapes,

twilight, salt breeze,
grace, birds foraging

among the leaves,
fine dust, fine chance …

then fire, far-
flung habits

dissolving
in a gust

Closed Intention

Since all beginnings
start from where you are—

the mirror, bewitched,
down-drift—these sly

selves sift the ashes,
document mysteries,

childhood, & the heavy shade
that comes before

the milk of morning,
where feathers collect

at the serpent's tail,
a great sigh rising

in the pulse of a breath,
waiting for the rain

to wash away the dream.

Revelations

Whispers, vespers
nestling euphoria,

answers to all letters,
a perilous tasklist.

Swear by all the rivers,
the cold cup of drought,

the summer's shimmer,
billows burning out,

setting toward the sun—
the longhand of the heart.

Glitters

The sky one may
remember, yet—

the dancers had
dairy feet, genders

clumping, night
was pulsing

& the shapes
of the outlines

against the canvas
equally at home

yet passionless.
Why should we live

in this sketchbook
loaded with desolations—

the danger of the mythical
dark, illuminated

only by suns
a zillion miles away,

& from those pinholes,
the silent birds

gawking
into the dome.

Inertia

Beyond the undulant,
in the half-life of dawn,

something wanders,
silent almost,

the cool air flowing over,
dissolving, delivering,

wrapped in the breath
of the underbrush,

shifting, materializing
in the hunter's eye, only

seconds before death.

45

Intolerable

Conditions of possibility,
systems of coherences,

constants, moralities of order,
a sense that knowledge is

knowing the codes of language—
tangled paths, secret passages,

strange, dark places
slithering in firebreathers,

sirens gathering before
that step into the flame ...

From a long way off
we look like flies.

Lost in the Z

Short Hand

Suggested possibilities—
enchanted, educated sacrifices,
realities one or two removed,
exams, personal nature,
prayer, secret admiration,
a feeling for love like
old meat, gagging, lost innocence,
obvious philosophies
under the stairs, scaring that living-
Jesus-out-of-me, the wheel turns,
God is praised by broken bread,
Sundays hear Him like lead, like
clanging, like worship, toast,
most of this can't be put
into words, the legend of youth
in & out of sermons, the devil's
weapon, a small thing well done,
snorting ninnies, belief,
faith, language mastered.
Gifts can be developed—or not.
Inspiration bumping along
in the cameo of small things,
in the shorthand of control.

Instructions

Go ahead. Demonize;
poetry is hardly a given thing.
Think. Step away.
I know it's unfashionable.
With the whole background
of history, the abyss that
divides perception, landmarks
of bad taste whipped into shape,
degrees of compassion hedging,
know how long the hunger holds,
mediocrities, sin, find out
something to change your life.
Faith? Good taste? Language
that fusses, a sense of what
words have become, work
on corralling the hardy ones,
go in, go out, what comes
easy is easy to believe, re-
order, write, real ideas are few,
exasperate, conflate, context-
ualize. Go ahead. Demonize.
There are serious problems
coming of age.

Obsessions

Christ, for Christ's sake.
Dead deep in high speech
the problems are never resolved.
What a wonderful surprise.

The Mechanism of Prayer

Split in the heart
until the third trimester.
Look up!
The mutters caught under the tongue,
the humdrum. Things never
said, the sounds, the bad
execution. Actually, the be-
ginning, the third eye,
a shell of life opens wide.
My bad education hanging
on a nail, transcendental.
That thing called love. God,
the investors calling. Moving
spiritual brochures, another
form of noise. If you can't
keep up, stand still. Visions
ahead, visions below.
The dread of heartbreak,
the dread of the Fall,
the dread of snow.

Truth

Mining the books
for hidden knowledge,
finding the secret,
the curious teaching
discarded, the end
of religion in one sense
or corrected in careless
improvisation. Inevitably
that teaching out of love,
the theme of intense
imagination. The barrage
of mindless hopes cannot
be denied. Trials, but no
celebrations—the strength required.
Walking the obvious,
a relief most difficult
to remember—details, some
sort of guru by your side,
being understood, no
words spoken in haste.
Pardon me. May we go on?

Full Effect

Mild? Sheer weight.
The clarity of choosing the dark.
Upset? Peel the skin,
look inside. Mysterious life.
Momentum. Insults.
Time, to be fair, dies
when language dies.
True poet, listen to your calling.
We *can* step forward
into a different sun.

Quite Resplendent

Honestly, analogies
are all signs, exaggerations
sifting out doctrine.

Spontaneous concern
invented a face & limbs.
Flat words for a fair boy.

Killing the snakes
to lie in the grass,
the death of someone beloved.

Little dribble from the wrong
end, learning on the job.
Disorganized? Danger?

Look, I'm growing younger.
This is my first assignment.
Devil in the detail.

The recording sounds like
someone, not your neighbor,
someone tragic. Spring comes

into its groves for a reason.
Put yourself
to useful work.

Dwelling

In anguished waiting.
Articulate condition
behind the eyes.
New order system,
lumbered purposelessness.
The mistakes of a long career
on the margins.

Rotten

Clods.
More public.
A subjective condition
depending on the weight.
Gurgling jargon
listening in
more than you thought.

Only the Future

In a sense
abandoning the muse.

Providing chaos
even past forty.

Heart-breakingly even.

Who has a right
to say that?

Defile. Deny.
Know your own extravagance.

To have begun
in mean feats

of hallucination.
To be hated?

Limp as a loose fish on the grass?

What is more terrible?
or more simple?

Don't forget that people
have learned to count.

With God Without

Doubt. No doubt.
Resilience in the state
of things. To give a damn
about. All the noble rage.
Exasperated. Devout.
All humans exist
from somewhere else.
Desperate circumstances?
No, the antithesis.
Happy it never worked out.

A Man Who Can't Explain

In Hell. Circumstances.
Dead? Accident?
Explaining everything away.
Embarking upon another journey,
it's true. The sun is
an accident. Dream outside
the dream. Prelude to
something else.

Calibrations

Hammering away the thought.
A manifestation,
a great mystery
lasting so long, long
enough at least
to contemplate God.
The truth of things,
new ways to love—
really not that far,
but fixed up like a king,
a masterpiece that defies
everything beautiful.
Is this the morality of humility?
We can become birds
in an act of love,
particularly when left
under a stone
babbling obscenities.
Naked technically
when something else happens
in the body. Were we such fools
to believe spiritual cohabitation
can be something else?

Half Truths

Read between the lines
with your nefarious mind.

Grammar isn't
what it's cracked up to be.

Look deep; stare; gawk.

Don't hold your breath;
there's something underlying all this.

Stop. Underscore.

A road half-traveled less
than more. Use it to reach

a pivotal performance.
Get your paycheck. The fallacy

of believing, therefore,
to be better, to be generous-

minded, right here
where all experience

performs, fishing for the
real American dream.

Oh, you so misunderstand.

A Curse

Remember
we are not of that breed.

We read far too much.
God is hectic.

Mechanisms today
select their own candidates.

Don't be afraid.

The greatest sinners
instinctively distrust

the boards as they walk
toward their imagination.

A fine, delicate touch
is all that is required.

Pull or Push?

It's all in the hands,
the choices.
                    Austerity
at the top of the hill.

Are you afraid to face it?

The distortion is pretty good.

Intrigue is often afraid
of itself.

Forty Feet High from Here

Tough choice.
Hullaballoo.
Scribble.
Rarely intelligent.
You know those simple stares
that cover up the mind.
Democracy is an entire force.
We have risky takes
on how fragile the concepts,
shedding the wrong answers.
He's right. Fearing who's
listening could cause
a psychic collapse.
Shoot straight.
Scribble.
Bugaboo.
Repose.

65

Anguished Nothings

Scarred. Jealous. Queasy.
Profound deep longing.
Caught in Socratic method.

Language swaggering,
discursive, disorganized
minds topping off likes,

squashing bugs & mites.
Hard pleasures rubbing
skin against skin.

Something like dying,
digging a hole,
publishing a book or two,

perpetual feeling of falling.
November rolls around,
then into winter, the right

to dance with the dead.
Struck flesh. Think.
Think again. Going down

but coming up (affairs)
at the top of the stairs,
thinking. Desperate.

Uncanny. A chill emerges
at the end of the dark.
Young blood, a burning

in the heart, throbbing.
A light flickers on. Mercy.
All the failures dissolve.

Unmitigated love,
& that less-than-you,
that possible-you, ignites,

that civilized-you crackles,
spits: "All will be done."
A cliché emerges.

On the intercom
a voice says: "Is that you?
Or someone else?"

Neolithic Age

Organized religion.
Creed. Noble rage.
"All the time" are God's words.

Why so far away,
that dull going-along-with-it?
I wanted to sleep

in the mud, alive
but apart. Think on it.
All these energies wrapped up.

Happy to meet halfway there.
Between my hands
a word never spoken,

never seen. Unconsciousness
buried in the exterior.
In the forest peopled

with leaves, the birds call:
"If only we could
swim in the deep."

Living the first day
of my life, re-living
the never-said. All visions

gone, but this, a world,
a world
dancing ahead.

OS ∞

01110100 01101000 01100101 01110010 01100101 00100000
01101001 01110011 00100000 01101110 01101111 00100000
01101111 01101110 01100101 00100000 01100101 01101100
01110011 01100101 00100000 01101001 01101110 00100000
01110100 01101000 01100101 00100000 01110111 01101111
01110010 01101100 01100100 00101110 00001010 00001010

there is no one else in the world.
there is no one else in sight ...

—The Google Brain AI-Bot

5 virtual Haiku translated from the Binary (AC2)

Buzzwords

It's so romantic
Hiding behind boulders & trees
Whipped up in foretaste

La Petite Mort

As-ifs that won't admit
The stories they tell us
Are serious & dangerous

Techno-Capitalism

History's freak show
Making probable claim on the future
Clones squeeze into old clothes

Live Streaming

Immaterial made material
Keeping my virtual reality
Intact in the black hole

Force of Nature

There is no demand
Under real circumstances
Scour at the table of exuberance

When We Come Forth & Walk

... at the end of the mind,
Beyond the last thought ...
The bird sings. Its feathers shine ...

—Wallace Stevens, from "Of Mere Being"

Sweet Colors

●

shadows
rekindled
in the grass
& in the murmur
of the trees
somewhere far off
evening opens

in the fans of corn
we see the faces
of the farmers & their wives
the buttercups plucked
wild behind their ears
& the deep umber
of dirt in the folds
of their summer dress

years burn away
into a single hour
of harvest
when birds come to watch
& stir the leaves
& the moon is
a schooner sailing away

●●

in the serene tone
just as on her own moon
the rocks change
their light
somehow already lost
on this spring
that endures
& that hesitating
upon the root
as if the acorn might
cradle the womb
of the earth
& then the sun smooths
the hairs, follicle by follicle
tender as if to a sickly child

here you want to smile
in reverie, resurge
then conceal
your life in autumn

●●●

in the wells
of the slopes
the wind of the woods
roving on the grasses

a sweet burn
that turns
on the naked shoulder

●●●●

that sleep in your eyes
islands once dwelt upon
innumerable seas
in the gleam of wings
a flash of light

open-handed child

the fruit of gods
beneath the tree

● ● ● ● ●

within the night, the floods
the green river
obscure blood
that has loved
in March, in flight
the young girls
beneath the hills

am I shuddering
in shades of words
only you recognize?

melt, Moon
September lives in the land

footsteps beat
upon broken stones

●●●●●/●

game that jars
the memory
the colored light
of summer

wasps
lamenting geese

the call of the snakes
in their nests

the trees
making up evening

in this trembling voice
the intimate joy
an age of sadness
yet still graceful
in the hip

meager fire
in the sky

●●●●●/●●

bread
like bread
sleep
like sleep
heavy heart but
stretching hands
rising swiftly, evenly
to the shore

●●●●●/●●●

drinking in
the dream

shipwrecked
in a consoled air

awake from the dead
in solemn stars

●●●●●/●●●●

isle-born
in the celestial fire

daybreak
quite undone by air

squalid exile
warm swamp

words & forms
in memory

◉

shadows & leaves
spoken

glad gust
of years & years

soft rain
the voice of trees

spirit of the floor

water

celestial heart
in the cell
deep light
in motion

beauty & sorrow
in the marrow of the bone

sinner
hear the sign

good work
in a sunken sun

sounding out
the dark

angels
awaken

a smile of hills & heavens
astray

take me in
soft motion
breathing in
years moaning out—

so light

live upon me
sulfur heart

make me the wind

the pain opening up
& easy to love
unshod, wavering
outpouring

make me blood

suffered
mutation

o patient day
abandon me
in silent houses—

no more dreams

drive me into the rivers
beat me speechless

grieve
dismay
reprieve

lunar waters
weightless, let me drift
into the clouds
behind the shipwreck

hurl me into the seed
weary of weight & sleep

repent

⊙ ●●●●●/●

what light
awakened me?

shapes of childhood?

skies travelling
in serene songs
revealing names
huddled, buried?

an eclipse
in whirlpools
of green reposes
rising—

first man out
outnumbered
in springtime

memory of death
breath, chill

rubble

⊙•••••/••

in vain
made sex again

new blood
fresh joy

beleaguered city
mirrored
in being-mine

deep breathing

Worldly Love

⊙●●●●●/●●●

furtive
fugitive
hanging mid air

unknown paths
opening wide
among the flowers

◉●●●●●/●●●●

among the flowers
celestial time

transfiguration

veins open
in the heart

awk-
ward

even-
ing

soft
islands

silen-
ces

sad-
ness

sky-
ward

seek me out
memory on water

winter
glory

in the midst of trees
morning air, behold
bold grass

voices open

drinking at the springs
the stars lift their wings

daily bread
not thin, still crude
squares

telephone pole—

vain
syllables, perhaps
in the heart

⊙⊙●●●

corroded days

water yielding
gardens

distant
voice

know all
that has not been
silent, square
houses, lowered
voices shimmering
recalling women
stone & sling

kill
kill the day

cover the heart

⊙ ⊙ ● ● ● ●

crumbled wall

love perhaps?

rivers of earth

leaves hanging
thunder hammering

image
overturned stone

accursed words
& the blind cloud

search
deep wailing
inscriptions

patrol

skilled

pass

search
among the dust

⊙⊙●●●●●

swollen feet
scratches of consent

surrounded
sounded

knee deep
soft senses

someone's alive
in the rubble

⊙⊙●●●●●/●

animals
held high

love floundering

move?

win if you will

wind does rise

what would you ask
if you were blind?

flourish

sunflowers
in the west

day I want to remember
within hands
like a flower

⊙⊙●●●●●/●●

the sunflower bomb
branches
silence

who denies
the trees?

what of their silent
solitude?

I know you are poor
so quick of the heart

mercy

false
my land is green

⊙ ⊙ ●●●●●/●●●

hair

flashes of metaphor
burn

april *is* false

⊙ ⊙ ●●●●●/●●●●

diary
in your face

trapeze

perhaps a game
in its every-
farthest-frenzied
instinct

happy waiting

irony loses it all

⊙ ⊙ ⊙

green-eyed
dialogue

Great Bear evening

hallucinating

growing with me every
where, everywhere
is stronger than men

smoke

howl
how centuries
of elegies
dawn against the target

arm's the measure

death, do not repent

the living
invisible

difficult attractions

shadows
who may, when
time, or perhaps
the light
ruptures
emerging

are not enough
for us

open the bridge
the switch is on

metropolis
from the stones

by the roots
of the world

years, men
likenesses

beyond
winter morning

amen

⊙⊙⊙●●●

measured December
along the rails

the science
in the dark

nothing else

darkly strong
difficult violet
threads of grass

hallowed heart
water drops
leaf has fled

canals, years, years

someone else will come
reveal the song
to the addressees

the poets, naturally

115

Then we came forth to rebehold the stars.
   —Dante, *The Divine Comedy*

Epilogue: Newton Releases a Little Bird Called Rocket

[Whoever is going to] make offerings
to the gods first [releases] for them a little bird,
[so that] he will come [welcome] to them [down there ...

—from the *Derveni Papyrus,* ascribed to Orpheus (5th century BCE), trans. Franco Ferrari (perhaps Europe's oldest surviving manuscript)

(1) Ignition

If science were raised
from the dead,

      or perhaps,
never dead at all—
           more a loop

returning to its beginning before
it ever ended,
             then the problem
of the one
      and the m a n y,

those shimmering paradoxes
wrung from the intuition
of unity
         (or the fountainhead

of the same myth)
      might be resolved
            in The Mirror of Being,

reflected back into the cycle in epicycle,

     the orb into the orb

of a mysterious circular motion

        that comes from an unknown center

—reaching those far-flung
island-flyspecks in the Pacific
between the Tropics

of Capricorn and Cancer

and the towering stone faces
                of giants

staring upon the expanse
of a lukewarm ocean.

(2) Burnout

Could it be that somewhere in the past
there was a soul who knew
what *In the Beginning* intimated?

And that someone terrestrial, but
peculiarly cosmic—
                    with the imagination
of an astrological power

found his armature of fingers,

counting those supernatural presences
    that plunged directly

        into the midst of things?

How many hundreds
of millions of years
were disrupted when you walked

across the bluffs,
    scraping the chalk
        from the underside
           of your muddy shoes?

How a fire in your hand
changed the world,

or, as Humboldt says:

First man will deny, then belittle,
then say he knew it all along.

(3) Coasting

From above the timberline,
our fugue follows a temporal order
manifest in the grinding

of the winds and her rains
upon all our visible surfaces;

and from within the maelstrom

a figure emerged,
                    an aura so numinous

it disguised the soul,
                ground,

within his own time,
                to peace and plenty:

from the twilight of the gods,
from the signs of life sprung from the sky river
or the greatest depths of a celestial ocean;

from the sidereal to the synodic,
the wave of arms that constituted
the histories of those who had come before—

in legend,
        in the alternate spaces
known as that dark, universal force
        of an original sin—

as if that might be the center of the thing.

(4) Apogee

A reason for living.

A reason for these lines of descent
and those religious excursions echoing
a holy order interlocked
in its own unity.
                And that everything
was a sign or signature of something else,

the metaphor being the meaning
behind matter and what mattered:

a code to be deciphered by those in the know—

what was once magic became mathematics,

the connections counted in the hologram
found the polyphony in a single quivering note.

Listening to the tuning of the sky,
                        the riddle,
                        a secret that could be unlocked

by applying thought to evidence—

the clues to which some divine creature
had strategically placed in the Great Wide Open.

There was no other reasoning with it.

(5) Recovery

Here was an unbroken chain of wisdom
handed down.
> The riddle would be revealed
to the initiate.
> The archaic spirit was clearly alive.

> > *How shall we speak*
> > *to those who are not yet born,*
> > says Galileo. *These are secret thoughts.*

Will someday two dozen signs
on a single leaf
seal the fate of man
as he sails upon an ocean
of milk churning to butter?

Afterword

"I think of myself as a kind of shaman, you know," Marc Vincenz once said to me, "communicating with the other side." I didn't quite know what he meant then, and probably mumbled something about Claude Levi-Strauss or Jerome Rothenberg, but reading *The Syndicate of Water & Light,* I think I finally understand. And I think, too, that it's appropriate that Vincenz made the revelation when we were in a dingy, black-walled Manhattan bar down below street level, where we went to wait out a heat wave that had engulfed the city. The place—dim and somehow squalid—had the feel of a kind of underworld, and it was of journeys to the underworld that Vincenz referred. This book is exactly such a journey, a voyage to another reality beneath our quotidian world, and, in the end, a journey back: a communication with the other side.

It is tempting, if one knows something about Vincenz's peripatetic and multilingual life, to trace an autobiographical story in *The Syndicate of Water & Light:* those teeming cities and markets ringing with exotic languages, surrounded by burgeoning industry, seem like the China where he spent a good portion of his life. And the pristine land of windblown grass, mountains, and sea could easily represent Iceland, where Vincenz retreated after a harrowing experience of venal modern Chinese klepto-capitalism. The sections dealing with Christianity, and a struggle to move beyond its formality to a more open view of the spirit, seem as though they may have come from his education in a Swiss monastery school, but I am cautioned against too autobiographical a reading here by Vincenz's statement that he arrived in the monastery an agnostic child and emerged a confirmed teenage atheist. Vincenz's life is present, here—how could it not be?—but it is refracted as if through a kaleidoscope, distorted and reformed into new patterns and symmetries.

The primary pattern is that of the expedition: the poem's presiding spirits, Ulysses and Dante, are both inveterate explorers. Significantly, they are not merely explorers of physical space, but seekers after knowledge—Dante's is a spiritual quest figured as geographic travel, and Vincenz' Ulysses is Tennyson's Ulysses, more than Homer's: the old mariner follows knowledge like a sinking star, sailing on to the shores of Mount Purgatory. Vincenz is an optimist, when it comes to journeys. *The Syndicate of Water and Light* opens with a sense that we can grow in knowledge and that we can change—if not, perhaps, the world, then at least ourselves:

> For more things are sought than found, they said.
> And after the fires of desire and delusion
>
> have been extinguished, observe the change
> of the roll and the pitch of the wave.
>
> What were the sources of our impulse?
> The what-we-don't-know-we-don't-yet-know?

For all this optimism, though, the journey will be a long one. The quest for knowledge begins with a sifting of codes and languages, a kind of post-Babel picking through the ruins. We see this throughout the book, but particularly in the poems of the first large section, "Where a Dark Bird Flourishes." Meaning is consumed in "whirling tongues of fire," and the one tribe that has seen Paradise cannot report back, the transcendent truths they witnessed remaining unspeakable. The mind is an "alphabet soup," we read, and we find ourselves lost: not just dislocated in space but in semiotic fields. Even our sense of our own identity becomes disrupted, and at one point Vincenz echoes Gertrude Stein, whose disjointed language and ambiguous identity were only grounded when she realized "I am I because my little dog knows me." Vincenz, at a point of intense confusion, breaks the fourth wall, telling us "here is where the dog enters/the poem & circles my feet"—a moment of respite in a journey that has already taken us far from our selves as we knew them.

The physical world of the journey is real enough, presented in moments of concrete particulars, but it is curiously without context. There are no proper nouns to name the factory towns and rivers rank with slurries of pollutants, here. And there are no sustained narratives to ground us in the lore of individual countries or traditions. Instead, we get a series of glimpses and fragments—flakes (to take an image from the book) in a shaken snow globe. There's a point to this. Matthew Arnold once said that we must strive to "to see life steadily and see it whole"—but Vincenz, like many moderns and post-moderns, believes we can only do one or the other, and he would see life whole rather than steadily. And this wholeness? Well, there's an implied world-system behind his fragments of landscapes and urban scenes, a system as destructive in industrial production as it is in consumer acquisition. The world of production, located in an anyplace or noplace, is:

impenetrable thicket
of pipes & tubes
of valves & bolts & flanges

& meters & dials pushing red,
of scaffolding & metal tanks
& columns of distillation bleeding

runoff into groundwater,
of effluents sweeping a paper-thin sky
where charred catwalks crisscross

an iced horizon ...

While the space of consumption, full of specific details but without a specified location, takes the form of:

our table wobbling under polyester flowers

or that faux fruit shimmering
on linoleum & the polyethylene tablecloths
fluttering a red & white checkered cotton

of olden French country cousins.
There the chemical fingerprints
where the origin of cancers beyond

the knowledge of science or
the market dynamics of a silent sea
surge …

  The outer journey is also an inner journey, and after a long night of the soul, in which formal religion yields to love and imagination (Vincenz has read his Romantics) we emerge to a healing space that is both inner and outer, physical and spiritual. In the twin sequences "Sweet Colors" and "Worldly Love," we find a pastoral landscape, a tranquil human love, and a semiotic simplicity, with "bread/like bread" and "sleep/like sleep." In the first of these sequences we are purged "speechless" beyond the "shipwreck" of the world, and we repent of our former sins. We have arrived at a kind of Mount Purgatory, on which we can ascend from the infernal depths of self-destruction and twisted love. In the second sequence we arrive at the simplicity of the world as it is—the fires of desire and delusion now in abeyance. We read of innocent pleasures like a "day I want to remember/within hands/like a flower." Codes and languages are simplified here, and we find ourselves out of the ruins of Babel. Indeed, we see a new order of symbols emerge in the numerical symbols that title the poems. It is important that the total number is 34: the exact number of cantos it takes Dante to emerge from his hellscape. It is important, too, that we end the sequences, as Dante does *The Inferno,* gazing upward at the stars.

The Syndicate of Water & Light doesn't end with these sequences, though. Like certain ambitious works of music, it concludes with a recapitulation of its themes. The epilogue, "Newton Releases a Little Bird Called Rocket," takes us to the stars we'd viewed, setting out on yet another a journey composed of phases both spiritual and physical: "Ignition," "Burnout," "Coasting," "Apogee," and "Recovery." The series links early avian offerings to the gods with space travel, implying that it is not just the poems of this book, but history itself, that recapitulates its perennial themes. This sense of a pattern behind the particulars of history and cultures may be the real treasure Vincenz takes home from his journey and lays at our feet in the form of a book.

—ROBERT ARCHAMBEAU

Acknowledgements

Acknowledgements are made to the editors of *The American Journal of Poetry, decomP, Hinchas de Poesia, The Journal of Poetics Research, New American Writing, Plume, Public Pool* and *Unlikely Stories Mark 5,* in which some of these poems previously appeared, sometimes in earlier versions. Many thanks to George Quasha and Sam Truitt, visionaries in poetic faith; and to Robert Archambeau and his meticulous critical eye.

About the Author

MARC VINCENZ is co-editor of *Fulcrum,* international editor of *Plume,* publisher and editor of MadHat Press and Plume Editions. He is the author of eleven books of poetry, including *Becoming the Sound of Bees* (Ampersand Books, 2015), *Sibylline* (Ampersand Books, 2016) and the forthcoming *Leaning into the Infinite* (Dos Madres Press, 2018). His novella set in ancient China, *Three Taos of T'ao, or How to Catch a White Elephant,* is to be released by Spuyten Duyvil in 2018. He has also been widely published elsewhere, including in *The Nation, Ploughshares, The Common, Solstice, Raritan, Notre Dame Review, World Literature Today, Los Angeles Review of Books, New World Writing,* et al.

Vincenz, who was born in Hong Kong and holds dual British and Swiss nationalities, is a multi-lingual translator of many contemporary German, French and Romanian authors. His latest work of translation, *Unexpected Development* (White Pine Press, 2018), by prize-winning Swiss novelist, poet and playwright Klaus Merz, was a finalist for the 2105 Cliff Becker Book Prize in Translation.

Vincenz has received fellowships and grants from the Swiss Arts Council, the National Endowment for the Arts, the Witter Bynner Foundation for Poetry and the Literary Colloquium Berlin. He lives in Massachusetts.

Other Works by Marc Vincenz

Poetry

The Propaganda Factory, or Speaking of Trees
Mao's Mole
Gods of a Ransacked Century
Behind the Wall at the Sugar Works (a verse novel)
Beautiful Rush
Additional Breathing Exercises
This Wasted Land and Its Chymical Illuminations (annotated by Tom Bradley)
Becoming the Sound of Bees

Limited Editions and Chapbooks

Benny and the Scottish Blues
Genetic Fires
Upholding Half the Sky
Pull of the Gravitons
Sibylline (illustrated by Dennis Paul Williams)

Translations

Kissing Nests by Werner Lutz
Nightshift / An Area of Shadows by Erika Burkart and Ernst Halter
A Late Recognition of the Signs by Erika Burkart
Grass Grows Inward by Andreas Neeser
Out of the Dust by Klaus Merz
Secret Letter by Erika Burkart
Lifelong Bird Migration by Jürg Amann
Unexpected Development by Klaus Merz
Casting a Spell in Spring by Alexander Xaver Gwerder

Fiction

Three Taos of T'ao, or How to Catch a White Elephant

CPSIA information can be obtained
at www.ICGtesting.com
Printed in the USA
LVOW12s1701030518
R13484400001B/R134844PG575200LVX1B/1/P